3/00

Shakespeare's Insults

for

DOCTORS

Books by Wayne F. Hill and Cynthia J. Öttchen

SHAKESPEARE'S INSULTS

SHAKESPEARE'S INSULTS FOR DOCTORS

SHAKESPEARE'S INSULTS FOR LAWYERS

SHAKESPEARE'S INSULTS

FOR

DOCTORS

WAYNE F. HILL

AND

CYNTHIA J. ÖTTCHEN

—

ILLUSTRATIONS
BY
TOM LULEVITCH

CLARKSON POTTER/PUBLISHERS
NEW YORK

Published by Clarkson N. Potter/Publishers,
201 East 50th Street, New York, New York 10022.
Member of the Crown Publishing Group.

Random House, Inc.
New York, Toronto, London, Sydney, Auckland

CLARKSON N. POTTER, POTTER, and colophon
are trademarks of Clarkson N. Potter, Inc.

Printed in the United States of America

Design by Alexander Knowlton
@ BEST Design Incorporated

Library of Congress Cataloging-in-Publication Data is
available upon request.

ISBN 0-517-70446–3

10   9   8   7   6   5   4   3   2   1

First Edition

This important little book
is dedicated to a sister-in-law and
a brother who are physicians,
and to another brother who is
a nurse. They feel compelled
to remain anonymous for reasons
of professional pride and politics.
But they are not alone in
lending authority to our work.
We also know people personally
who have actually been treated by
doctors, and we once considered
having it done ourselves.
The thought was bizarre enough
to inspire this unprecedented and
uniquely important travelogue
through the medical world.

He will be the physician

that should be the patient.

TROILUS AND CRESSIDA

CONTENTS

INTRODUCTION

> Of course everybody lives
> in perfect health forever.
> Or we *would*—it's only the
> doctors who don't let us.
> Physicians make an art of
> pretending they know more
> than we do, but the real
> problem is that they know
> lots more than they say.
> They're holding out.

In times past we gracefully accepted infirmity as inevitable, and we did it by an admirably early age. But the rising tide of medical progress so increases our suspicions that we needn't be unwell. It's our bygone youthful graciousness, then, that doctors are helping us to recover. Often this is the only recovery being offered, but even we must admit that the alternative is intolerable. We would not want it on our consciences that we contributed to making the present situation worse: the uncontrollably multiplying medical advances of the twentieth century have encouraged everyone to demand an instant cure for every half-imagined twinge. But physicians simply haven't the energy. As a consequence, they courageously take up the thankless task of lowering expectations.

We all sympathize with the doctors, but medical science has not come this far only to be withheld from us. Claim your fair share of progress before the lights go dim. Let them have a piece of your mind. Never fear giving offense, for nothing you say is taken personally anyway, doctors being professional as they are. They'll look upon you as scientific research, but you'll feel doubly improved for having donated to a charitable cause.

Cast illusion aside. Medicine is not a mutually beneficial project for perfecting natural bodily functions. It's an invigorating conflict, a spirited exchange. Medicine is literally cut and thrust, tooth and tong. And who better to raise the level of medical invective than Shakespeare? He knew conflict. His 38 plays contain nearly ten thousand of the world's most cultivated insults. The testy bits chosen for this seminal collection stimulate both sides: for doctors to give and for doctors to get.

Take up the sword, if not the caduceus. If doctors would only do something for us, we'd be fine. But most of the time they say they can't and make us feel bad about it. Doctors already hold a tremendous advantage. People have been prevented from living forever for a very long time now. But we needn't take it lying down.

Doctors deliberately set a hellish stage. While they chill their icy hands, we're shut half-naked in subarctic examination rooms that reek of cheap alcohol, left to our fate in the menacing presence of dog-eared magazines from 1987. No one could feel fit under such circumstances. The doctor suddenly appears, pokes, thumps, and pinches, mumbles fat Latin syllables and scribbles hieroglyphic prescriptions for eye of newt, toe of frog, and then—*poof*—disappears. It's the doctors who scare the life out of us, who give us the mortifying names for things. Were it not for medicine, we hypochondriacs wouldn't know what to imagine.

Doctors thrive on the invasion of privacy. In that crucial moment when a near-stranger is plying up and down our spine, when the gown goes up or the lights come down, we might find ourselves at a loss for words. That's when we'll need a bit of a prompt. Some poetry. That's the time for Shakespeare.

Shakespeare has a scalpel tongue, a laser wit. He puts us in the doctor's costume, strides right in and cuts through the platitudes. It's *attitude,* not anatomy. *Bodies,* not biology. *Candor,* not catheters. He transforms every aspect of medical practice into the social intercourse it really is. Shakespeare's opinion of doctors is well known. One has already expired before *All's Well that Ends Well* even begins, and his young daughter proves the better doctor anyhow. In *The Merry Wives of Windsor,* a distinguished Continental physician doesn't quite win the maiden's heart. Upon such indisputable cultural authority this book collects Shakespeare's insults for the breathtaking, heart-throbbing, gut-wrenching, knee-jerking, toe-sucking world of medicine. If we must be humbled by the latex hand, we can hold on to our dignity through the diction of the master who, as we know, is famously immortal.

ON DOCTORS

[You] lay on

like a butcher.

HENRY V
5. 2. 144

OLD HABITS DIE HARD (pardon the expression), but modern medicine's traditionalism could do with a bit of livening up. Conventional wisdom, received in medical school, holds that patients actually *like* their doom pronounced in dulcet tones that discourage argument. This practice is misguided. It inhibits the doctor's sincere desire to express real feelings about us, and it sedates us when we could be storming against the heavens, as Shakespeare might say.

Actually euphemism, like rheumatism, botulism, or the flu, is an illness. The Bard prescribes a cure: purging the wit. Calling a doctor a mechanic slave, for example, accelerates the pulse. In the excitement, we'll either go sooner, but much more gratified, or live ten minutes longer on sheer momentum. If we've had a particularly dull life, this could be our finest hour. Be ready when the doctor grows suspiciously gentle.

*You starvelling, you eel-skin, you dried
neat's-tongue, you bull's-pizzle, you stock-fish
—O for breath to utter what is like thee!—
you tailor's-yard, you sheath, you bow-case,
you vile standing tuck!*

HENRY IV, PART 1
2. 4. 240–44

He shall think it fit to expound
his beastly mind to us.

CYMBELINE
1. 7. 150—53

Come, come, you talk greasily;
your lips grow foul.

LOVE'S LABOUR'S LOST
4. 1. 136

Thou hast the most unsavoury similes.

HENRY IV, PART 1
1. 2. 77

[You are] a sort of tinkers.

HENRY VI, PART 2
3. 2. 276

[You are] like an envious sneaping frost
That bites the first-born infants
of the spring.

LOVE'S LABOUR'S LOST
1. 1. 100—1

To die by thee were but to die in jest.

HENRY VI, PART 2
3. 2. 399

I perceive but cold demeanor.

JULIUS CAESAR
5. 2. 3–4

O, I smell false Latin.

LOVE'S LABOUR'S LOST
5. 1. 75

*He draweth out the thread of his verbosity
finer than the staple of his argument.*

LOVE'S LABOUR'S LOST
5. 1. 17–18

*[You] are only reputed wise
for saying nothing.*

THE MERCHANT OF VENICE
1. 1. 96–97

Thou disease of a friend!

TIMON OF ATHENS
3. 1. 53

*How dares thy harsh rude tongue
sound this unpleasing news?*

RICHARD II
3. 4. 74

[You have an] undressed, unpolished,
uneducated, unpruned, untrained,
or rather unlettered, or ratherest,
unconfirmed fashion.

LOVE'S LABOUR'S LOST
4. 2. 16–19

THE HOSPITAL EXPERIENCE

HOSPITALS ARE INSTITUTIONS. They come straight from a bureaucrat's fondest dream—byzantine, with rules of iron, and germ-free. Hospitals are always touted as designed for our superior care, but they actually exist for the convenience of doctors. The evidence is indisputable: house calls diminish significantly when all the patients are under one roof. There's no physical impossibility in simply bringing a CAT scanner to our doorstep, what with people back from the moon decades ago. But somehow simple things always prove difficult where administrators thrive.

As a distraction, hospital supporters (who are usually politicians, alias bureaucrats) often compare their hospitals with hotels that offer every amenity—with service hand and foot. We wonder if a more candid comparison might be with the airlines. All airplanes smell the same. There are lots of little buttons to push. Someone in uniform is always nearby to tell us what not to do. Space isn't literally cramped, but almost, and the food isn't literally edible, but almost. And once we're in, we always look forward to getting out, whether we will or not.

While airline travel is a more modern invention, Shakespeare obviously had at least secondhand knowledge of such full service institutions, where "brethren and sisters of the hold-door trade" were in abundance and where foreign bodies, among other things, leapt from bed to bed.

If the cook help to make the gluttony,
you help to make the diseases.

HENRY IV, PART 2
2. 4. 44–45

[You] pernicious blood-sucker
of sleeping men!

HENRY VI, PART 2
3. 2. 225

*Put thy face between his sheets and
do the office of a warming-pan.*

HENRY V

2. 1. 83–84

I have purchased many diseases
under her roof.

MACBETH
1 . 2 . 42–43

Peas and beans are as dank here
as a dog, and that is the best way
to give poor jades the bots.

HENRY IV, PART 1
2 . 1 . 8–9

Most ungentle fortune
Have plac'd me in this sty,
where, since I came,
Diseases have been sold dearer than physic.

PERICLES
4 . 6 . 95–97

Thy food is such
As hath been belch'd on by infected lungs.

PERICLES
4 . 6 . 167–68

DOCTORS HUMILIATE US by declaring what is wrong with us, but the numbing effect is short-lived. They know that the most effective way to render us docile and undemanding is to enlist us as participants. They give us something mildly ridiculous to do. Follow this regimen, spread on that paste, ingest unfailingly every four hours on the dot some pellet, capsule, pill, or concoction. Once we're being silly, we've lost the self-assurance to stand up for ourselves.

All this is ancient superstition anyway, like eating warrior's heart *tartare* to cure cowardice. Shakespeare adapts this very practice to propagandistic ends in the aptly named (medically speaking) *Much Ado About Nothing*. However sweet "eating a man's heart in the marketplace" might taste to a vivid woman like Beatrice, in the recent more gracious past the beneficent powers of medicines were guaranteed by their bitterness. Cod liver oil, for instance, disgusted whole generations anxious to cure, apparently, some inability to swim in alcohol or eat heaps of questionable cheese (to which discomforts cod livers are naturally immune).

Today unpleasantness remains essential to securing our cooperation, but now the term "bitterness" has been redefined, through petrochemical research, to mean "wild cherry flavored" or "pleasantly tasting of orange [chalk]," as all medicines today do. By mouthing Shakespeare's liberating insults, though, we learn to trust our own taste.

*Such boil'd stuff as well
might poison poison.*

CYMBELINE
1. 7. 125–26

*The bitterness of it I now
belch from my heart.*

CYMBELINE
3. 5. 137–38

*I were better to be eaten to death
with a rust than to be scoured to
nothing with perpetual motion.*

HENRY IV, PART 2
1. 2. 219–21

[He] sweats to death,
And lards the lean earth as he walks along.

HENRY IV, PART 1
2. 2. 103–4

"THE BEST THINGS IN LIFE are free" has been discredited as utter nonsense, but this good-feeling platitude goes some way toward explaining why insurance companies exist. Month by month, we unconsciously transfer huge premiums to the insurers for nothing tangible whatsoever. Then, when some bodily hitch catches us off our guards, the company uses our money to fight against our claims, loses the fight, and then pays the doctor enormous wages to pat our hand and prescribe a placebo. And for all this attention, we can tell overselves we aren't paying a penny. We're covered. Life simply doesn't get better than this.

Still, we're obliged to protest against the doctors for making their zillions. Shakespeare's insults, at the very least, help keep visitation charges down.

I do desire we may be better strangers.

As You Like It
3. 2. 254

[These are] diseas'd ventures that play with
all infirmities for gold.

CYMBELINE
1. 7. 123–24

If I hope well, I'll never see thee more.

TIMON OF ATHENS
4. 3. 173

[You] can get no remedy against this
consumption of the purse.

HENRY IV, PART 2
1. 2. 237–39

[He will] something lean to
cut-purse with quick hand.

HENRY V
5. 1. 90

ON PATIENTS

What strange ruins may we

perceive walking [here]?

THE TWO NOBLE KINSMEN
1. 2. 13–15

ABETTED BY DOCTORS, spreading like a fashion through the developed world, the ever more muscular physical fitness movement keeps expanding. But hardly anyone asks, "Fit for what?"

The lords of fitness have domesticated manual labor by introducing the workout. The trick of adapting it to grasping, semipolite society was turned by disconnecting work from productivity. (All that huffing and puffing doesn't blow the house down.) And rather than being paid a pittance like their sweating prototypes, fitness participants themselves often pay enormous sums for the privilege. Objectively, the end of those million workouts is nothing, if not less than nothing. (Notice our restraint in that we have not mentioned, and will not, the old out-of-breath argument that joggers merely increase their exposure to being run over by beer trucks or delivery vans full of cigarettes.)

Doctors who champion fitness have upset the natural order: get sick, go see the doctor. Natural orders tend to reassert themselves vigorously if not violently. If we get sick *after* seeing the doctor, it's obviously the doctor's fault. Blame will be justly heaped upon the prevention doctor who fails to prevent. These are dire consequences, rather than the easy admiration hoped for. Perhaps physicians haven't thought their position through.

These same doctors have also blown a whistle on culinary pleasure, by restricting diet. However, every schoolchild knows that eating is its own reward. If the body were meant for health food there would be tastebuds for blandness and they would go all the way down. But flavors are savored in the organs of speech, and all the doctor's tasteless talk of calories and cholesterol won't stand up to the poetry of a single dollop of chocolate. Diet-and-fitness doctors have got something wrong.

All this is more than mere unsupported opinion. In a major recent study scientists took all the most popular diets recommended by doctors for optimum human health, averaged them, and compared the result to unspoiled nature. The conclusion was potentially explosive. The one creature in the wild that most naturally follows all our best-selling doctors' orders is the hippopotamus. The results of this study have been suppressed, of course, but it is perhaps more unfortunate that an authority like Shakespeare is required to put all this into perspective. If everyone were perfectly fit, he would have had less to say about people, and the human race would be deprived of one of its keenest observers.

[You're] but a filthy piece of work.

TIMON OF ATHENS

1. 1. 199

*His days are foul and his
drink dangerous.*

TIMON OF ATHENS

3. 5. 75

*This unwholesome humidity,
this gross watery pumpion.*

THE MERRY WIVES OF WINDSOR

3. 3. 35–37

His guts are made of puddings.

THE MERRY WIVES OF WINDSOR

2. 1. 31

[Your body is a] muddy vesture of decay.

THE MERCHANT OF VENICE
5. 1. 64

Thou idle immaterial skein of sleave silk,
thou green sarsenet flap for a sore eye, thou
tassel of a prodigal's purse, thou:
ah, how the poor world is pestered with such
water-flies, diminutives of nature!

TROILUS AND CRESSIDA
5. 1. 29–33

Why, thou globe of sinful continents,
what a life dost thou lead!

HENRY IV, PART 2
2. 4. 282–83

[He] shall die of a sweat, unless already
he be killed with your hard opinions.

HENRY IV, PART 2
EPI. 30–31

[You are] full of bread and sloth.

THE TWO NOBLE KINSMEN
1. 1. 158–59

Chang'd to a worser shape
thou canst not be.

HENRY VI, PART 1
5. 3. 36

*[They] have so strutted and bellowed
that I have thought some of Nature's
journeymen had made men,
and not made them well.*

HAMLET
3. 2. 29–34

*God made him, and therefore
let him pass for a man.*

THE MERCHANT OF VENICE
1. 2. 53

*Wherefore waste I time to counsel thee
That art a votary to fond desire?*

THE TWO GENTLEMEN OF VERONA
1. 1. 51–52

*[Your] breath stinks with
eating toasted cheese.*

HENRY VI, PART 2
4. 7. 10–11

*[You are] a great eater of beef, and I believe
that does harm to [your] wit.*

TWELFTH NIGHT
1. 3. 84–85

They must be dieted like mules,
And have their provender
tied to their mouths.

HENRY VI, PART 1
1. 2. 10-11

A stone-cutter or a painter could not
have made him so ill, though they had been
but two years o' th' trade.

KING LEAR
2. 2. 58-60

DIAGNOSIS

IF ART OUTRUNS SCIENCE at any point
in medical practice, diagnosis is where it
happens. Some doctors have an uncanny
nose for maladies. These high priests of the
flesh bring their arch powers into fathoming
our phlegm, divining the slurred language
of our livers.

Most physicians, of course, have the sim-
pler gifts of mere mortals. But not to
despair. Doctors can rectify the unjust distri-
bution of talent by adding a few stock gen-
eralities to that perfect kneecap-jellifying

He is no less than a stuffed man.

MUCH ADO ABOUT NOTHING
1. 1. 53

forehand smash with their rubber mallets. They can work on becoming the Nijinskys of stethoscope placement and leave the rest to the Bard.

We have collected a repertoire of Shakespearean diagnoses that can lend you doctors that all-important aura of genius. No matter what symptoms may appear in the patient, simply shout out any one of the following Shakespearean assessments. This method will serve as well as any usual technique. You will certainly avoid being known as ordinary. And for those doctors who hesitated between veterinary and human medicine, we have even provided one highly adaptable diagnosis inspired by warm sentiments for the nobler forms of life you left behind. Perhaps some of you will notice which one it is.

He is lousy.

ALL'S WELL THAT ENDS WELL
4. 3. 188

This effect defective comes by cause.

HAMLET
2. 2. 103

Thou worms-meat in respect of a
good piece of flesh indeed!

AS YOU LIKE IT
3. 2. 63–64

You are as a candle,
the better part burnt out.

HENRY IV, PART 2
1. 2. 155–56

[He is] possessed with the glanders and like to
mose in the chine, troubled with the lampass,
infected with the fashions, full of windgalls,
sped with spavins, rayed with the yellows,
past cure of the fives, stark spoiled with the
staggers, begnawn with the bots, swayed in
the back and shoulder-shotten, near-legged
before, and with a half-cheeked bit and a
headstall of sheep's leather, which, being
restrained to keep him from stumbling, hath
been often burst and new-repaired with knots.

THE TAMING OF THE SHREW
3. 2. 48–58

[You] diffus'd infection of a man!

RICHARD III

1. 2. 78

Thou dost infect my eyes.

RICHARD III

1. 2. 152

[You] owner of a foul disease!

HAMLET

4. 1. 21

You are as rheumatic as two dry toasts.

HENRY IV, PART 2

2. 4. 55–56

Were I like thee I'd throw away myself.

TIMON OF ATHENS

4. 3. 221

Poor worm, thou art infected.

THE TEMPEST

3. 1. 31

I will begin at thy heel,
and tell what thou art by inches!

TROILUS AND CRESSIDA

2. 1. 50–51

[You're] a fusty nut with no kernel.

TROILUS AND CRESSIDA
2. 1. 103–4

PROGNOSIS

MEDICINE IS A MINOR BRANCH of the art of fortune-telling, falling between derivatives trading and horse racing. Those practitioners who predict eventual mortality are merely cowardly—if not guilty of fixing. And those who mumble "There, there, everything will be all right" are blindly betting the bank. Shakespeare lends intellectual vigor to the sport of prognosis.

*He'll yield the crow a pudding
one of these days.*

HENRY V
2. 1. 87–88

*She [has] as many diseases as
two and fifty horses.*

THE TAMING OF THE SHREW
1. 2. 80

*It appeareth nothing to me but a foul
and pestilent congregation of vapours.*

HAMLET

2. 2. 301–3

Go rot!

THE WINTER'S TALE
1. 2. 324

You'll be rotten ere you be half ripe.

AS YOU LIKE IT
3. 2. 117

You are polluted with your lusts.

HENRY VI, PART 1
5. 4. 43

Much uncurbable, her garboils.

ANTONY AND CLEOPATRA
2. 2. 67

Our crows shall fare the better for you.

CYMBELINE
3. 1. 83–84

Make thy sepulchre,
And creep into it far before thy time.

HENRY VI, PART 3
1. 1. 243–44

Throw this slave upon the dunghill.

KING LEAR
3. 7. 95–96

You breathe in vain.

TIMON OF ATHENS
3. 5. 60

With the help of a surgeon he might yet
recover, and prove an ass.

A MIDSUMMER NIGHT'S DREAM
5. 1. 298–99

Give me your hand. I can tell your fortune.
You are a fool.

THE TWO NOBLE KINSMEN
3. 5. 74–75

A pox damn you, you muddy rascal,
is that all the comfort you give me?

HENRY IV, PART 2
2. 4. 39–40

DOCTORS ARE NOT THE ONLY ONES worthy of criticism. They sometimes do have reason to be horrified by patients who suffer a lapse in humankind's otherwise unblemished record of excellent behavior. These seldom-seen apparitions haunt doctors not because they love doctors too little but because they love them too much. They actively seek medical advice (an obviously ill-considered enterprise in itself), but worse they want it free. Family members (including former in-laws and distant cousins), neighbors, old nearly forgotten acquaintances, old completely forgotten acquaintances, childhood pals, friends of former friends, deliverymen, and total strangers are among the more notorious for wanting free advice—even though we have already proved that nothing is free and that such a craven attitude sacrifices self-respect for nothing.

With dignity all spent, the patient from hell is driven to complain. But complaining and insulting are entirely different matters.

One is unimaginative and dead-ended, while the other is life-giving and retort-inviting. Shakespeare despises the whiner even as he arms the righteous for verbal assault. In the end the patient from hell is someone who is uncooperative, stubborn, and rude with a churlish imagination twisted toward hypochondria. Although this may sound like a calmly considered description of modern industrialized humanity, remember that the Bard lived before our era and that his insults already are appropriate to such figures. In other words, apparitions must they be, for they surely are not we.

Wilt thou on thy death bed play the ruffian,
And seek for sorrow with thy spectacles?

HENRY VI, PART 2
5. 1. 164–65

[I] must not break my back
to heal his finger.

TIMON OF ATHENS
2. 1. 24

[You] great-siz'd monster of ingratitude!

TROILUS AND CRESSIDA

3. 2. 147

The tartness of his face sours ripe grapes.

CORIOLANUS
5. 4. 17–18

Talk thy tongue weary.

CYMBELINE
3. 4. 114

I am merrier to die than thou art to live.

CYMBELINE
5. 4. 143

*Be thou the sullen presage
of your own decay.*

KING JOHN
1. 1. 127–28

Farewell, sour annoy!

HENRY VI, PART 3
5. 7. 45

Pig-like he whines.

THE TWO NOBLE KINSMEN
5. 4. 69

[You are an] ingrate and canker'd.

KING HENRY IV, PART 1
1. 3. 135

Steep this letter in sack and make him eat it.

HENRY IV, PART 2
2. 2. 128–29

Go thou and fill another room in hell.

RICHARD II
5. 5. 107

*[You are] a good lustre of conceit
in a turf of earth.*

LOVE'S LABOUR'S LOST
4. 2. 86–87

*He is so plaguy proud that
the death-tokens of it
Cry "No Recovery."*

TROILUS AND CRESSIDA
2. 3. 178–79

I'll beat thee, but I should infect my hands.

TIMON OF ATHENS
4. 3. 366

I have said too much unto a heart of stone.

TWELFTH NIGHT
3. 4. 203

What cracker is this same that deafs our ears
With this abundance of superfluous breath.

KING JOHN
2.1.147–48

He receives comfort like cold porridge.

THE TEMPEST
2. 1. 10

He's compos'd of harshness.

THE TEMPEST
3. 1. 9

Now the rotten diseases of the south, the guts-
griping, ruptures, catarrhs, loads o' gravel
i'th'back, lethargies, cold palsies, raw eyes,
dirt-rotten livers, whissing lungs, bladders
full of impostume, sciaticas, lime-kilns
i'th'palm, incurable bone-ache, and the
rivelled fee-simple of the tetter, take and take
again such preposterous discoveries!

TROILUS AND CRESSIDA
5. 1. 16–23

SPECIALISTS

Mere prattle

without practice.

OTHELLO
1. 1. 26

SPECIALIZATION IS PROOF of how far medicine has skidded off the path. No longer is it a matter of people stimulating one another's nerves and wit's ends. We can no longer simply be ill or injured. No, as the cart pulls the horse, so knowledge now drags along the doctors. And this great careering sledge piled with ever-doubling information compels doctors to claim, incredibly, that not one of them knows enough about every-thing to do something. It lets them abandon heaps of medical expertise to sluggish igno-rance in the way farmers dump excess pro-duction to keep prices up. That is the genius of specialization: an ability to claim general non-knowledge.

Further, the humblest doctor can now make a name, not by making us feel better or by saving the President, but by piling more facts into the cart. This creates a prob-lem for ordinary sick people. With plenty already to watch out for, we now must beware of the knowledge-engendering doc-tor who might be pushing a very unumbili-cal fibre optic up our navel for a few snapshots to illustrate his latest theory for the glossy medical journals. We must be certain to secure worldwide royalties before undergoing even a local anesthetic, while our modest little abnormality is curing medicine of its alleged ignorance. In actual fact, ignorance is a chimera. Doctors know enough and always have. If proof is even required, the proof is that 400 years ago one person, William Shakespeare, was able to converse intelligently over the whole range of medical endeavor. And he could do it without so much as being aware that he was doing so.

Although modern medicine knows enough to make us all brilliantly youthful forever, the doctors hold back. And although they do not need a piece of our mind, they by their own specialization have issued an open invitation. We humbly oblige.

GENERAL PRACTITIONERS

Thou clay-brained guts,
thou knotty-pated fool, thou whoreson obscene
greasy tallow-catch.

HENRY IV, PART 1
2. 4. 221–23

Bid them wash their faces,
and keep their teeth clean.

CORIOLANUS
2. 3. 62–63

I'll carbonado your shanks.

KING LEAR
2. 2. 38

Nature disclaims in thee:
a tailor made thee.

KING LEAR
2. 2. 55

A plague on them, they ne'er come
but I look to be wash'd!

PERICLES
2. 1. 25–26

What have we here?
a man or a fish? dead or alive?

THE TEMPEST
2. 2. 24–25

[You are] but a filthy piece of work.

TIMON OF ATHENS
1. 1. 199

[You are] mechanic slaves
With greasy aprons, rules, and hammers.

Antony and Cleopatra

5. 2. 208–9

If he were opened and you find so much blood
in his liver as will clog the foot of
a flea, I'll eat the rest of th' anatomy.

TWELFTH NIGHT
3. 2. 58–61

BRAIN SURGEONS

His brain is as dry as the remainder biscuit
after a voyage.

AS YOU LIKE IT
2. 7. 38–40

Not Hercules could have knocked
out his brains, for he had none.

CYMBELINE
4. 2. 113–15

I'll make a quagmire out of
your mingled brains.

HENRY IV, PART 1
1. 4. 108

Thy brains
[Are] useless, boil'd within thy skull.

TEMPEST
5. 1. 59–60

Thou hast no more brains
than I have in my elbows.

TROILUS AND CRESSIDA
2. 1. 45–47

His pia mater is not worth
the ninth part of a sparrow.

TROILUS AND CRESSIDA
2. 1. 73–74

[He] wears his wit in his belly
and his guts in his head.

TROILUS AND CRESSIDA
2. 1. 75–76

INTERNAL MEDICINE

Thou art a boil, a plague-sore, or embossed
carbuncle, in my corrupted blood.

KING LEAR
2. 4. 225–27

I would not have such a heart in my bosom,
for the dignity of the whole body.

MACBETH
5. 1. 52–53

He has not so much brain as ear-wax.

TROILUS AND CRESSIDA
5. 1. 51–52

Fat-kidney'd rascal.

HENRY IV, PART 1

2. 2. 5

[You are] white-livered and red-faced.

HENRY V

3. 2. 33

Foul indigested lump.

HENRY VI, PART 2

5. 1. 157

Pigeon-liver!

HAMLET

2. 2. 573

PROCTOLOGISTS

*[This is] the rankest compound of villainous
smell that ever offended nostril.*

THE MERRY WIVES OF WINDSOR

3. 5. 82–84

Doth thy other mouth call me?

THE TEMPEST

2. 2. 98

Thou art so leaky
That we must leave thee to thy sinking.

ANTONY AND CLEOPATRA
3. 13. 63–64

[You] ruinous butt.

TROILUS AND CRESSIDA
5. 1. 27

Out, dunghill!

KING JOHN
4. 3. 87

[You are] a resolved villain
Whose bowels suddenly burst out.

KING JOHN
5. 6. 29–30

When all's done, you look but on a stool.

MACBETH
3. 4. 66–67

His forward voice, now, is to speak well
of his friend; his backward voice is
to utter foul speeches and to detract.

THE TEMPEST
2. 2. 91–94

Your bum is the greatest thing about you.

MACBETH

2. 1. 214–16

Your means are very slender,
and your waste is great.

HENRY IV, PART 2
1. 2. 139–40

I could wish he would
modestly examine himelf.

MUCH ADO ABOUT NOTHING
2. 3. 200–1

Thou thing of no bowels thou!

TROILUS AND CRESSIDA
2. 1. 52

Why, this hath not a finger's dignity.

TROILUS AND CRESSIDA
1. 3. 204

OSTEOPATHS

They have all new legs, and lame ones.

HENRY VIII
1. 3. 11

Thy best props are warped!

THE TWO NOBLE KINSMEN
3. 2. 32

Thy bones are hollow; impiety
has made a feast of thee.

MACBETH
1. 2. 52–53

Aches contract and starve your supple joints!

TIMON OF ATHENS
1. 1. 247

Depender on a thing that leans.

CYMBELINE
1. 6. 58

DENTISTS

My bended hook shall pierce
Their slimy jaws.

ANTONY AND CLEOPATRA
2. 5. 12–13

Teeth hadst thou in thy head
when thou wast born,
To signify thou cam'st to bite the world.

HENRY VI, PART 3
5. 6. 53–54

We had like to have had our noses snapped
off with old men without teeth.

MUCH ADO ABOUT NOTHING
5. 1. 115–16

I will give thee bloody teeth.

ANTONY AND CLEOPATRA
1. 5. 70

Chill pick your teeth.

KING LEAR
4. 6. 246

EYE, EAR, NOSE, AND THROAT

All the infections that the sun sucks up
From bogs, fens, flats, on [him] fall, and
make him
By inch-meal a disease!

THE TEMPEST
2. 2. 13

Thy lips rot off!

TIMON OF ATHENS
4. 3. 64

By this hand, I will take thee
a box on the ear!

HENRY V
4. 1. 221–22

I durst not laugh, for fear of opening
my lips and receiving the bad air.

JULIUS CAESAR
1. 2. 246–47

Three times was his nose discharg'd against
me; he stands there
like a mortar-piece to blow us.

HENRY VIII
5. 3. 43–45

Art thou the slave that with
thy breath hast kill'd?

MUCH ADO ABOUT NOTHING
5. 1. 257

A pox o'your throat, you bawling,
blasphemous, incharitable dog.

THE TEMPEST
1. 1. 40–41

[You have] a blasting
and a scandalous breath.

MACBETH
5. 1. 125

DERMATOLOGISTS

A most instant tetter [scab] bark'd about
Most lazar-like, with vile and loathsome crust.

HAMLET
1. 5. 71–72

I never see thy face but
I think upon hell-fire.

HENRY IV, PART 1
3. 3. 29–30

[Your] face is not worth sunburning.

HENRY V
5. 2. 150

I would thou dids't itch from head to foot:
and I had the scratching of thee, I would
make thee the loathsomest scab in Greece.

TROILUS AND CRESSIDA
2. 1. 27–29

Scratching could not make [a face] worse,
and 'twere such a face as yours were.

MUCH ADO ABOUT NOTHING
1. 1. 126–27

O flesh, flesh, how art thou fishified.

ROMEO AND JULIET

2. 4. 38–39

Thou crusty botch of nature!

TROILUS AND CRESSIDA

5. 1. 5

PLASTIC SURGEONS

[What a] slovenly unhandsome corse!

HENRY IV, PART 1

1. 3. 43

Sell your face for five pence and 'tis dear.

KING JOHN

1. 1. 153

*Thou wert best set thy lower part
where thy nose stands.*

ALL'S WELL THAT ENDS WELL

2. 3. 247–48

*[I'll] scotch [you] and notch
[you] like a carbonado.*

CORIOLANUS

4. 5. 191–92

I have seen better faces in my time
Than stands on any shoulder that I see
Before me at this instant.

KING LEAR
2. 2. 94–96

How foul and loathsome is thine image!

THE TAMING OF THE SHREW
IND. 1. 33

I will beat thee into handsomeness.

TROILUS AND CRESSIDA
2. 1. 15

Your face is a book where men
may read strange matters.

MACBETH
1. 5. 62–63

PSYCHIATRISTS

Would the fountain of your mind
were clear again, that I might
water an ass at it.

TROILUS AND CRESSIDA
3. 3. 308–9

My friend, carry your tail without offence
Or scandal to the ladies.

THE TWO NOBLE KINSMEN
3. 5. 31–32

*[You] blunt monster with
uncounted heads!*

HENRY IV, PART 2
1. 0. 18

*[You act] with great imagination
proper to madmen.*

HENRY IV, PART 2
1. 3. 29–30

*Some strange commotion
is in [your] brain.*

HENRY VIII
3. 2. 112–13

[You're] a dull and muddy-mettled rascal.

HAMLET
2. 2. 562

*You have some sick offence
within your mind.*

JULIUS CAESAR
2. 1. 268

You recount your sorrows to a stone.

TITUS ANDRONICUS
3. 1. 29

Thy rage shall burn thee up,
and thou shalt turn to ashes.

KING JOHN
3. 1. 270–71

[You are] a fellow o' th' strangest
mind i' th' world.

TWELFTH NIGHT
1. 3. 110–11

He speaks nothing but madman.

TWELFTH NIGHT
1. 5. 106–7

O, you are sick of self-love and taste
with a distempered appetite.

TWELFTH NIGHT
1. 5. 89–90

SEX THERAPISTS

In his sleep he does little harm,
save to his bedclothes about him.

ALL'S WELL THAT ENDS WELL
4. 3. 246–48

Is it not strange that desire should so many
years outlive performance?

HENRY IV, PART 2
2. 4. 258–59

This mock of his hath turn'd
his balls to gun-stones.

HENRY V
1. 2. 281–82

Small things make base men proud.

HENRY VI, PART 2
4. 1. 105

Thou misshapen Dick!

HENRY VI, PART 3
5. 5. 35

[You] poor inch of nature!

PERICLES
3. 1. 34

CONCLUSION

IN CONCLUSION, WE MUST NOT FAIL to suggest the rich possibilities of bringing the genius of Shakespeare into the art of psychosomatics. This is the enviable gift of being able to stage whole repertory seasons of tragi-comic maladies in the theater of one's own involuntary flesh. The excellence of this achievement lies in attracting large numbers of physicians to attend the gala openings. The proper standard is not merely creating convincing symptoms but producing such a confusing combination of them as to reflect deep truths of contemporary culture and inspire genuine shock and perhaps even bafflement. This is what all of today's great artists do.

Any of the Shakespearean diagnoses we have included in this medical handbook can be used to stimulate wonderfully imagined self-engendered illnesses. By employing the vivid language of the Bard, the ordinary patient or even the aspiring patient can work new layers of complexity into the art of unhealth.

Doctors, too, can practice a colorful psychosomatism by freely covering up the elusiveness of any illness by attributing it to a mere crank idea wedged up in a blockhead.